CAMPAIGN BATTLE

2022 (Second edition)

Legal Disclaimer

This book is designed to provide information and motivation to our readers. It is sold with the understanding that the publisher is not engaged to render any type of psychological, legal, or any other kind of professional advice. The content of each chapter is the sole expression and opinion of its author, and not necessarily that of the publisher. No warranties or guarantees are expressed or implied by the publisher's choice to include any of the content in this volume. Neither the publisher nor the individual author shall be liable for any physical, psychological, emotional, financial, or commercial damages, including, but not limited to, special, incidental, consequential or other damages. You are responsible for your own choices, actions, and results.

CONTENTS

Chapter 1: Introduction

Politicians need to be crafty ba$tards; they need to be inspired by the past but learn to adapt to changes in a very dynamic environment. To be successful, one should learn how to fully utilize tools such as trending policies, media and religion to influence the masses. In this book, I will attempt to give you the dirty tricks strategists use to enable a specific candidate to gain the momentum needed to be elected and analyze how they work in conjunction with the factors within the election process.

A lot of what people see is just a mask. Politicians just have to appear in a certain way, that's just how it works. The concept given to voters is vital in gaining their support and if it doesn't look like a politician has vision, no one is going to vote for them. It needs to get people excited, promise something better than what they already have. It is like a business proposal; however, politicians are not making a deal at this point, they are just looking for your attention.

A candidate's true beliefs don't matter. Don't get me wrong, of course, they have beliefs, but if they want to win, they often need to put these beliefs aside. The most important thing about campaigning is to be relevant and understand what masses want NOW. It doesn't matter what the political situation was five years ago or even a year ago. What might have been relevant back then might never be spoken about again. Politicians can potentially contradict themselves because they are juggling so many different positions. If they want to win, they have to 'sell their soul' and go completely against their gut instincts. It's the price of power.

The average voter is naive and doesn't understand why all their wishes and demands can't be met. They expect a lot for minimum commitment and because of this, there is a lot of room for manipulation by the political machine. Also, many people rely on only a couple of sources of information and do not question them. Their pool of information is limited which leaves them to make generalizations and false (or over-exaggerated) conclusions about the political situation as a whole.

It's not just about core voters and swing voters. You have a wide range of people involved in the political process: families and friends, people in the country and people in the city, students, brain surgeons and financial brokers. There are a variety of views that have developed over time or have been influenced by their specific surroundings, which means that they might be very fractured in what they think and believe. It's the strategists' job to put all these puzzle pieces together, faster than the other side and explore how this data can be used in the best possible way.

Candidates have got to read the voters and see what their mood is. By keeping neutral ground candidates can develop a better understanding of the political situation and play it to their advantage. Otherwise, they are limiting themself and not accepting reality. Politicians that are too extreme will only attract extreme voters. Although this may be a strategy for those who aim to just represent a particular group or belief, this won't win them the popular vote.

Ideology clash

The difference in ideologies is always going to be a thing in politics. And since politics is an inevitable part of life itself, there is no situation where there is no clash of ideologies. If there is no imminent conflict, a situation could arise as people are pushed to extremes because of the lack of representation of their opinions (or partial representation of their opinion).

The strength of ideology is heavily connected with the power structure of the political system. For example, a centralized government is where the decisions within the country are taken by a small group of people, so there are not many clashes because the leadership is powerful enough to silence any opposition groups and voices.

On the other hand, having a multiparty system might mean the power is more decentralized and the decision making is distributed among more branches. Having such structure, though, can lead to a more serious clash of ideologies depending on how divided the voters are. This, in turn, could bring the country to a political crisis or new elections.

A two-party system could also resemble either of the two extreme scenarios above. The two parties basically have a monopoly on the voters, and they control most of the political spectrum and can silence ideas outside of their scope. But when they are divided in almost equal measure and disagree on a major issue, it could cause a political deadlock and consequently, even a government shutdown.

No political system is better than another, they all have pros and cons based on the circumstances. Here are the three possible scenarios to consider during the election process and how they are related to ideological struggles:

• **One-party system** - The party has total dominance over different points of view or can easily oppress ideological differences and shut down other people's opinions.

• **Two-party system** - There are two major parties controlling the course of the country and ideology is split between the two. They can ignore minor voices that do not match their political agenda.

• **Multi-party system** - In cases of a heavily fractured political landscape, some parties might arise that stand behind a single issue. Blocks can be formed to act like a two-party system, but a new election cycle will be needed if consensus is not found.

Ideologies usually start out with good intentions or at least 'perceived' good intentions. However, when practices associated with certain ideologies are implemented, they can become something quite different from what was envisioned. Parties evolve and not always in a good way. This is usually more strongly expressed when the extreme wings of parties take over leadership. This acts as a corrective measure to return to the principles of the party ideology, when the party stretches too far from the course they originally envisioned. When the narrative goes too far, the political message can become toxic for the mass public and only a small group of extreme people approve of its continued implementation. One thing is for sure; it's always difficult to get the reasoning behind policies across to 'the other side'. People will never completely understand each other!

Chapter 2: Equilibrium Palette

The general principles might vary under different political situations or social environments. For example, you can't apply the same rules on a country on the brink of civil war and a country that is relatively stable, the results will not be the same. In an extreme environment, the outcome is expected to be extreme, but it doesn't mean it can't be predicted. The 'rules' explored in this book, as explained, are open to the possibility of being wrong or slightly skewed.

Let's start by saying a few words about the concentration of power and how this affects the players involved in the political process. Heavy centralization and authoritarianism is a way to control by effectively putting all the decision making of a country under one person. This is not always a forceful process and it can sometimes be the result of an election. Such power structures make decisions easier because there is no opposition to conflict with, but at the same time, they can seriously limit the rights of the people.

On the other hand, a fragmented political landscape and too many players involved in decision making can block important changes and gridlock can emerge where the country stagnates, unable to move past an issue. To make the situation harder to deal with, some groups may attempt to use their leverage to go against the consensus of the leading party on any issue just to say 'I am here and you have to acknowledge me', causing problems simply for the sake of getting the electorate's attention.

Sometimes it is better to win the people first and think about policies later, but this is not always an option on the table. Some strategists even make up policies as they go along, taking risks on the way. In this chapter we are going to largely focus on analyzing the main players in the process, political figures, the money behind them and the voting masses, 'the People'.

Candidates

The dirty truth is that there are only two viable choices of candidate: 'fanatic' or 'liar'. If they truly believe in their ideology, a candidate will be a radical defender of the concepts they believe in, a 'fanatic'. On the other hand, 'liars' are more likely to have flexible personal opinions but project views they know will rally up and excite the core electorate.

Though there are two types of candidate, there is an additional option which can transition to one of the other two options.

- **Liars** - Someone with flexible ideological views that can publicly fluctuate based on the other candidates around them and the party agenda.

- **Fanatics** - Hardcore believers, often with a background in activism. They are more likely to truly believe in the ideology they represent.

- **Naive** - They are largely non-radical, optimistic and principled candidates, but are unelectable unless someone powerful is behind them or they politically evolve to one of the first two types.

However a candidate is categorized, one of the most important things for an electable candidate to have is charisma. The main thing a voter notices about a politician is how they speak; people often connect it with leadership. Holding the interest of a small crowd is not enough though, a winning candidate should be able to be charismatic on a big stage. However, charisma is not just about being able to speak in front of large groups of people, it is also the ability to hold a conversation and steer it to a topic they want to talk about.

To have a successful candidate, charisma is a must and political strategists need to choose from the three options mentioned above. All other personality traits are extra and could benefit or damage the candidacy to some extent.

Another important distinction to make between candidates is are they a 'career politician' or a 'non-career politician'? In other words, have they made a name for themselves as a politician or elsewhere? This can be important depending on the situation. Sometimes non-professional politicians might strive and there are times where they are basically non-electable. This might be the result of the political and/or cultural environment, state of the economy or geopolitical relations. Coming from a background away from politics can help candidates appear more counterculture and human, while the career politicians can suffer from looking like robots. An interesting life feeds into the illusion that anyone can become a leader, an illusion of freedom which can be appealing to voters.

Electable candidates project credibility and appear resourceful. They should look like 'doers', able to deliver and resolve issues. A 'liar' candidate can usually get more out of an election, usually being more appealing to the average voter (of course, they will likely not think of the candidate as a liar). For the most part, such candidates can recognize and understand other points of view and they have the ability to be flexible, not just preaching to their party base. Under different circumstances, though, they would be completely capable of defending other ideologies as easily as they can defend the party they are presently involved in. You know, being consistent is not the same as being honest.

The issue with the other primary type of candidate - the 'fanatics' - is their extreme position on issues which stems from their extreme ideology. They usually have a tough time campaigning to swing voters and moderates. Fanatic candidates tend to garner their own core voters over time which can enable them to promote themselves within the party or even start their own countermovement.

Independent candidates without the support of a major party can't have a serious impact on elections. Yet, by participating they will have a stage to make some noise and potentially share different points of view. 'Naive' candidates, although rare, are basically a preceding stage of the 'liar' type of candidate. 'Naive' candidates are usually moderate, non-fanatics that would like to do 'the right things for the right reasons'. They usually have a strong stand on issues they care about and are not ready to defect from their original position or flip to a different ideology, even when this could be politically beneficial for them. For such people to be electable, though, they should be recognized by the establishment as their champion. Then, 'naive' candidates can quickly evolve into 'liars' if they want to last long enough to have a chance of fighting for at least some of the policies they care about. The political battlefield is the ultimate place to corrupt anyone.

Regardless of the political system, political dynasties are always a thing in any country. The families of those in power are well-known, yet they don't necessarily have more of a chance of gaining power themselves. They are not necessarily charismatic, but it is very likely that they have connections to support a potential 'jump in the race' and perhaps even some experience because of the family they were born into. A candidate's background should also be considered. Are they war heroes, activists? Even the people that work from them might be an issue for the upcoming battle. A candidate's health level is also important for the average voter. If for instance, a candidate looks like they are at death's door or simply appears too old (even if they are not) it can be a game-changer. Health issues might hit a campaign very hard.

That leads us on to more shallow attributes which can be used as a tool; the physical attractiveness of candidates and of candidates' families. Statistically speaking, voters are drawn and willing to accept more attractive people. On top of that, tabloid newspapers and magazines tend to write a lot about this subject - after all, to some degree, they are celebrities. Journalists and bloggers will write all kinds of gossip and will discuss their clothing and lifestyle. Depending on the interests of the tabloid or magazine, this can have either a positive or negative effect on building voters' opinions on candidates.

Regarding the families of candidates, people will ask questions about them as it helps some voters build a bigger picture of their personality, history and achievements. All members of the family should be well-to-do-with. Ideally, they should have good jobs, be decently educated, project a stable family, be married and ideally have a few kids, and it is also important to ensure that this image is maintained. If a candidate cannot control their family, how can they control a country? The image of their family can sometimes be just as important as the candidate themselves. Sometimes even extended family will be looked into as well. The media and opposition will be looking into ways to find dirt on them, anything. In general, it is a must for the strategists to be able to put a spin on bad news or make it not relevant.

Voters

It is vital to profile and understand the different types of potential voters in the election process. Gaining supporters is more complicated than just being a nice person and people start liking you. It is largely to do with what voters are looking for themselves and what they believe (certain purposes, such as, political, religious, etc.). On top of that, there are other factors influencing them - the state of the economy, national crises - and sometimes they vote according to what they think is most suitable to their lifestyle.

It's also not like starting from 0 and working your way up to 100%. Some things are already in place depending on who is backing the candidate, such as their party or other organizations. It usually comes down to maintaining and improving that initial percentage. And even if candidates can't get any more voters, they need to make sure they don't lose what they already have.

Voters can be divided into three primary groups:

•	**Core electorate** - Core voters are loyal party followers and heavily driven by ideology.

•	**Swing voters** - They are liable to change their mind and usually don't self-identify with any specific political party or ideology.

•	**Cause-driven voters** - Such voters can follow a specific ideology but narrow in on specific topics. To them, political parties do not matter much as focusing on an issue close to them.

Core voters should 'look like' they are a candidate's most important voters. They are the voters the campaigners know will most certainly vote for their candidate regardless of their actions. That said, if the candidate does not belong to a dominant political party, it is highly likely that they will not have such a group of people behind them. This is because most core voters are attached to the beliefs that are supposedly associated with that particular party. The most frequently observed relate to the political 'left' and 'right'.

One of a candidate's primary responsibilities is to keep votes secured within their party. It is possible to lose these voters if candidates actions sway too far away from the party's agenda. Though it is also highly unlikely that the opposition will win these lost votes, by losing them in the first place candidates are strongly diminishing their chances of winning. Core voters can often be found in specific regions that are known to vote in a particular way. However, this should not be counted on and there is a risk of losing such domains of support. Deprived of their own core voters, the candidates can't win the election.

Essentially, swing voters are trend followers whether they know it or not. The biggest battle for candidates is to get swing voters on their side. However, campaigning strictly for swing voters is dangerous as candidates might appear to be drifting away from party principles and this risks losing core voters who may feel left out, as mentioned above. That said, even when the party has most of a voter's boxes ticked for policies, it is sometimes not enough. Swing voter's interests can be incredibly varied, and they can vote over very small issues or even one specific issue that bothers them. Some may only be concerned with issues within their own geographical area. Not all swing voters are sheep that can easily be herded into your pen. Cause-driven voters might vote more tactically, and it can be difficult to track or persuade them.

Cultural movements should always be taken into consideration by candidates and strategists. To be successful, they must follow trends and be aware of rising counterculture movements, regardless if they support them or not. If they manage to catch the wave, it could be a great advantage over their opponents, giving them the freedom to act accordingly and appear relevant to the mass public. In the end, counterculture always gets absorbed into mainstream culture. What was considered counterculture a few years before may be considered normal today. If strategists want to take this approach, they must bear in mind, mass cultural opinions change and they need to keep track of them. Counterculture can belong to any part of the political spectrum - left, right or center.

There will always be people looking to rebel against 'the system' and they can never be fully removed. If they're removed, others will simply appear in their place. They will always feel that they are fighting injustice or for a specific issue to be heard. Two things can be done with these people; one, use their argument when it suits a candidate's agenda, two, steer clear of them when their support could lose the candidate's middle ground in the election.

General voter's attention is a funny thing, it can last long or it can fade away fast. It depends on the way that they are pounded by information, which can be influenced by different media's affiliations to parties and policies. The public's opinion can swing dramatically because, generally, they are not looking at all the facts, they can end up cherry-picking certain bits of information or only have access to specific points of view. If a major scandal happened last year or even a few months ago, voters' interest can wane. Usually, voters only care about scandals close to major events, which on the other hand are fueled by the people who control paths information. Even the largest mistakes can be forgotten if the candidates or the party backing them up are powerful enough.

To have a better grip on the election process, besides general campaigning, candidates should target particular groups of people or even entire industries and address their problems. The leaders of communities or respectable companies are influential public figures and by praising or pledging support to a candidate it can spark interest for many potential voters. Policies can be introduced to show how the candidate will help them flourish. In theory, better functioning industries and government organizations can mean better standards of living.

Every society has its subculture groups. They may share similar beliefs though they can be divided along some ideological lines. Demographics play a big role in the way political parties approach potentially new voters or deny their opponent's access to the communities they have a stronger influence on. The political struggle, especially when the race is tight, often pushes a party's ideology too far in one direction, which can lead to forms of discrimination finding a place in their platforms. One group of people openly having more rights than the rest or discriminating against large portions of society can seriously shake the stability of a country, which increases the possibility of tension, violence and even increasing the likeliness of separatists movements emerging.

Party HQ

A major party is a powerful structure and a major source of decision-making in any campaign battle. The people orchestrating the campaign, strategists, party leadership or the candidate themself should be able to recognize the party hierarchy, people holding key positions and people with some sort of leverage. Usually, this is more strongly expressed in the dominant mainstream parties that have likely been around for a while. There is a huge difference between established parties and 'one-season' parties that might be driven by a one-time event or specific individuals (well-known faces, celebrities for example).

No party is ever going to be completely united. There will be different groups dedicated to specific causes or that have alliances with one another. To have a better chance of winning, the majority of these groups have to back a single candidate. However, gaining the support of the vast majority of party members is only the first step of succeeding. The candidate also needs to be able to silence or distance themself from the people they believe will be harmful to the campaign.

Trust is vital to establish in the early stages. Some people are more likely to align with the agenda and have a common ground with the candidate. On the contrary, the process of distancing from certain groups and individuals can be risky. They might deliberately start sabotaging and undermining any progress made. People can be bitter, no one wants to be sidelined and some might be more powerful than anticipated.

The establishment of the party can keep control by following the three steps below:

•   **Stop voices against the party's donors** - With no money, it is impossible for the party to launch a successful campaign.

•   **Don't allow voices different from the party agenda gain the upper hand** - Divisive viewpoints might split the party from within.

•   **Stay firm against the major opposition party** - If voters consider two opposing parties one and the same, many will look for an alternative.

People within the party who disagree with the ideas displayed within the campaign need to be silenced. There are two primary ways to get their backing; either buy them off if they are a 'liar' or by promising to back some of their critical ideological ideas if they are a 'fanatic'. There is a third option of sabotaging them when everything else fails by making them look foolish or extreme. They need to be smeared but carefully, otherwise, you risk giving them a platform to oppose you.

It is natural for the establishment to fight against change, but they should be able to recognize cycles and trends in order to survive. To be a candidate backed by a party, one must come from either the party's status quo or have a serious background in a specific industry such as a business tycoon or from a well-known dynasty. The establishment should have a filter to stop inconvenient candidates who don't tick all their boxes. Party leadership can change the rules to stop unfavorable candidates. If candidates are not restrained, they could potentially take over leadership of the party and have party members united around them.

Additionally, political parties are almost always linked to some organizations or groups of interest, sometimes even entire industries. A source of money! It can be devastating for a party if a candidate starts fighting against convenient policies for their big donors. It can be hard to cancel a candidate who has serious resources backing them, as mentioned earlier, everything comes down to money. To counter imminent threats like new players, the establishment should consolidate for their own good against them and then eventually be flexible enough to incorporate different voices.

Usually, the extreme wings of a party are the most dangerous to mingle with. A candidate's potential alliance with such groups can even split the party. Radical voices within a moderate party can scare voters and push them away. Speaking up against radical fractions should be done in a timely manner.

Back to the election process, party leadership might prefer one candidate over another. Though blocking 'dangerous' candidates usually means more control over the party structure by the establishment, core voters (and even some swing voters) can be pushed away. Selecting a non-career politician candidate is also a risky move for the party structure, as its leadership has less control over them. Expectedly, candidates who have nothing to lose can afford to be more controversial because they have other options in life (rich, famous, etc.). Career politicians don't have this freedom as they have invested too much time to reach this point and many have dedicated their entire working life to politics.

Upcoming and energetic 'new faces' pose a threat to the establishment if the party is in crisis, fractured or facing bad electoral performance. Upon a successful campaign, a candidate might unite the party under themself, change the party structure and even potentially shift its ideology and focus. The interesting thing about political parties is that even when they thrive in a so-called democracy, their structure is extremely top-down. The question is: who is going to be at the top?

The team behind the campaign should also be politically convenient and strategic. For instance, choosing the right running mate: the 'team' should be built to fit with the ideology that has been created around the campaign, but the political surroundings shouldn't outshine the primary candidate. Candidates often ally themselves with other key party members in an exchange of favors that could come in many forms, such as giving them a particular role in the cabinet, passing or relaxing certain laws, or business-related activities. What these people receive should depend on the amount of power and influence they can assist with.

Big money

In some countries, the law regulates the sum of donations coming from one source, however, one way or another, money will find its way into politics. The donors of a candidate's opponent are their true enemy. Money is the fuel of any campaign, if concentrated and combined with power, it can heavily influence any election. Follow the money and you will be able to forecast the policies and legislation to come. This is especially relevant for big donors, as they can control whole sectors of the economy.

Money talks, no large success is possible without key resources behind a campaign - corporate donors, small donors or other organizations:

• **Big-donors** - Large businesses and even entire industries as a source of money. Funds are raised to prevent the implementation of policies and legislations, usually dictated by special interests.

• **Small-donors** - Individuals and small-business owners as a source of money. Funds can be primarily raised by campaigning and controlling paths of information (media networks for instance).

• **Foreign agents** - Foreign governments and organizations as a source of money. Their goal is usually to destabilize or cement to power a party or a candidate.

In one-party political systems, businesses can be heavily controlled or owned by the government. Yet, the principle stays the same: find out where the money is coming from and you will understand the logic behind any legislation. In heavily centralized governments, though, big money is just a tool, not the source of policies. Money and politics go hand to hand.

In order to ignite small-donors enough to put money on a campaign, they need to strongly believe in an ideology or strongly oppose a contrasting one. Mass support from small donors can occur, but usually only in cases where widely unpopular policies are being pushed that they do not agree with. Mass support from small donations means an accumulation of a huge amount of money, which can create a formidable political force. This, in turn, can conflict with the interests of some large donors as they are often the reason for pushing policies too far. Big donors are after something very specific related to the industries they work with or own, while small donors are mainly concerned about factors that affect their lifestyle or beliefs.

Small donors can feel more inspired if the candidate feels marginalized or at least portrays themself in that way. For this to be seen, a candidate needs to appear on paths of information (access to mass media channels). Without a stage for mass exposure, the fundraising impact is limited. Alternatively, candidates can hold campaign rallies and other events. Interestingly, it doesn't matter whether media channels are privately owned or state-owned, someone still controls the media it delivers, basically making them 'content gatekeepers'.

The big difference between being funded by small-donors rather than big-donors is that because the source of donations is more decentralized, theoretically, candidates have more freedom, bearing in mind that they still need to follow some lines of the party HQ. Similarly, when the big-donors donate directly to the campaign they have less control, but when they donate to the party, this is a whole new story. In such situations, candidates are expected to follow and change policy positions accordingly.

Those that represent the strongest industries of an economy have a higher capacity to lobby. Big-donors can lobby more effectively when oligarchs and elites have an industry monopoly. They can have a huge influence on the decision-making process and typically push for tax cuts, government contracts, and policy change, for example.

A potential conflict may arise when big-donors' interests go against party ideology. The image of publicly aligned campaign backers needs to be effectively judged in order to avoid scandals or a backlash from core voters. Additionally, when a candidate takes money without fulfilling donors' expectations, they will likely seek revenge which can cause various problems.

Chapter 3: Puzzle Pieces

There are certain cycles or tendencies that repeat themselves during most elections. Of course, they don't always happen in the same way, but to a certain degree look similar. By understanding the core principles of these cycles, strategists can be better prepared to react, enabling them to be more flexible and able to change their plans accordingly.

The balance of power of any country is a result of the political situation or how power is divided between the actual rule makers and the branches of power. The biggest player might not have complete control and might need the support of other people and organizations, who are on their side of the aisle and sometimes who are not on their side.

In a sense, a successful campaign means to build a 'mythology' around the candidate and make it feel more like a movement than an election to energize the voters. Facts, for better or worse, are not always as important as fitting into an idea. Having a strong mythology can make a campaign appear more formidable in comparison to its competitors. Strategists need to be very specific about the attributes they would like the campaign to have. If it is too similar to their opponent's, voters can lose interest in the candidate and maybe in the whole voting process.

Everything must relate to the culture of the targeted voters and transcend any short-term trends. That said, polarizing voters can have a positive effect on the election result as it sometimes shows strong points of view and character, which can help a candidate stand out. The bottom line is: outrage sells well! This might be a dangerous game though, special benefits for specific groups of society might easily bring unrest and disappointment for the majority of voters.

Politicians don't just need to pick their battles and use questionably moral tools, but they need to create them in order to give themselves an unfair advantage which can be looked upon as an achievement. This chapter is dedicated to the most common tools used in politics.

Media

Any publicity can be good publicity if you use it the right way. Media is not just an accumulation of events, there are a lot of variables that can affect how candidates are portrayed. Usually, the media hides its own interests. There are rules, but they change depending on who is using the media. Ideally, the candidate's agenda should align with the media's own agenda. Like driving a car, they need to find the best way to operate it. While it might be useful, it could inflict self-harm to the whole campaign, if not driven correctly.

There are three rules that drive the media's focus and determine how it will be operated:

•   **Donors' interests** - Media owners may have specific interests. For example, if an industry owns a media outlet, they may try to push their agenda, which can affect public opinion.

•   **Ratings** - Also important because media companies sell ratings to advertisers before everything else. The more viewers they have, the more power they have.

•   **Being unbiased** - Being unbiased is only possible when it does not contradict the first two rules.

The primary reason the media exists is to be the center of attention and aggregate attention. Candidates and the media use each other, even when they are on opposite sides of an argument. The process has two sides; to build 'useful' archetypes for their chosen candidate or to create a narrative that could be harmful for their opponent. The latter option can backfire in the hands of those who wanted to use disinformation or manufacture a hoax. In such situations, it's possible that they end up boosting support for their opponent, especially when it looks like the media is attacking them. However, as long as people are buying into it, it will make an opponent look foolish or damage their credibility.

In a one-party political system, people are often stuck to limited sources of information, such as a single channel for state media. On the contrary, a multi-party system with a lack of government centralization and regulation can create conditions for a media monopoly to form, which depending on the situation could be the best or the worst thing to happen to a candidate (given the party supporting them and their special interests).

To get better exposure, more attention and higher ratings, the media predominantly seeks out the extremes. At the same time, in the eyes of the viewers, good news and bad news is like a pendulum swinging back and forth. And when a media outlet is unable to balance between the special interests behind them, exciting news and the political environment as a whole, everything could backfire in a mass withdrawal of viewers, resulting in a rating drop. If the narrative goes too far when attacking opponents, the media actions could even start damaging the candidates they are supposed to back.

While censorship does not only exist in dictatorships, strategists should find a softer way to 'silence' voices against the establishment when the system is not heavily centralized. This could be accomplished by the media boycotting events related to inconvenient political ideologies, ignoring or even banning candidates and activists. However, repeating propaganda messages over and over again will only have a positive effect on a campaign until it crosses a line and goes too far from popular positions, losing credibility in the eyes of the vast majority voters.

Handling only 'convenient' stories for a certain candidate is also essentially propaganda. The media can also be used to manipulate news about a candidate's opponent by creating misleading bombastic headlines about them, typically with legal phrasing that can protect them from lawsuits hidden somewhere in the article. Strategists can politically weaponize rumors or even manufacture scandals if they have nothing solid to build their attack on. When defending themselves from attack, candidates need to counter bad news with good news or direct attention to a less damaging topic. More recent news usually outweighs old news. It's all about how a story is framed, focused on or if it is vague and out of context.

If candidates don't have the media on their side due to party affiliation or interpersonal relations, they need to find creative ways to gain more exposure and draw attention to themselves. An interesting resemblance between candidates and the media is that they are both after ratings and it is vital for them not to be 'forgotten' by the people. Publicity is always costly and should be achieved on a mass scale, which would require state or private resources, affordable predominantly for prosperous and influential people with power. Smaller players need to go along with the media's rules, or they may end up negatively portrayed or simply blacklisted. A message might be the same for most candidates, though, the way it is presented can be different.

Public figures, famous hosts, comedians and satirists can be seen as alternative paths of information for campaigns. When their message is linked to widely accepted policies the impact can multiply.

Activists

Extreme movements can find their place under any ideology. Moderate activists are rare because they usually are indoctrinated core voters. The political purpose of active members is to imply to the mass public that a specific ideology or policy is socially acceptable and becoming a new norm.

Even if it might look like there are many of them, in reality, there are only a few. Their size is usually perpetuated by the media who are always looking for a new story, which is often something to agitate people. Most people actually don't care too much about politics and even if they do, they have to carry on with their daily lives and work. They simply don't have the time to engage their minds and dedicate resources to politics.

Making use of activists is a balancing act. A candidate would probably want them on their side but not want to be too aligned with them because empowered activists can scare off moderate voters. Further to that, politicians are not in complete control over what activists may do and if they are too publicly linked to each other, there might be a negative impact on the candidate's chances.

To fully utilize an activist movement related to a party, there are several requirements:

•   **Capacity to engage and convince** - Activists are a candidate's feet on the ground, to push for causes related to the party. They can be a great propaganda tool because their social activeness draws a lot of attention and that can present their actions as a new norm.

•   **Using them wisely necessitates keeping some distance** - Activists should have energy, not power. Their impact should be limited because they can take over the party.

•   **Pretend their opponents are all extreme** - Candidates can use extreme movements associated with their opponents to paint their entire party as extreme.

Activists can be politicized without them realizing they have been used. These people are the 'real believers' driven by principles, passionate but often fanatics, unfortunately. Activists believe their arguments and actions are convincing, but in fact, the true use of them is to intimidate and sometimes scare opponent's voters. These are not the guys that candidates need to win, they will most likely vote for their side of the political spectrum anyway.

A candidate should find a way to fuel radical movements to intimidate others without being connected to them too publicly. If a scandal emerges, a candidate might even disavowal them, yet not act too strong upon them or take further action to stop them. Throwing activists under the bus might be necessary if the scandal is too high profile and there is a risk of losing voters.

When activists join a candidate's cause, they are basically embodying them, becoming one with them in a sense. They are a cheap propaganda tool budget-wise because they are driven by ideology. Ideally, candidates would like to have activists angry when bad things happen to them and to protest if their agenda is hurt. Activists should be given stage exposure, without it they are not activists, but just emotional core voters who cannot be seen.

Generating a movement usually starts from an idea, but it could also start from a person if the candidate is very influential or charismatic. Once they reach a necessary level of dedication and readiness to live for a cause, activists will most likely remain loyal to a candidate forever, but they must believe that the candidate truly believes in their cause.

Pushing activists too far can be a really dangerous game. Letting them loose is usually only implemented when everything else is lost and winning looks impossible. It is a desperate move that in some cases might even start a revolution. At this point, public perception of the candidate is probably immensely deteriorated, and they have possibly even lost core voters on the way. When the candidate is fully linked to the hardcore wings of the party, any distance in association is evaporated.

To radicalize activists and make them berserk is an extreme step. The further they go to the extremes, regardless of the party they align themselves to, the more alike they are in terms of aggression and unwillingness to accept views other than theirs. Emotion becomes aggression when lines are crossed.

Even when they are not extreme, activists on the other side can also be used in the election process. The more radical the opponent's activists look the better choice the candidate looks for the swing voters. If the opposition party backs their extreme wings, they can be easily attacked because they are defending an extreme ideology. The candidates should point this out and make the voters believe that everyone on their opponent's side is the same.

Aggressive activists shouldn't be mistaken for angry voters. They are just ideologically disappointed people who are not actively involved in social causes, and they cannot be used as efficiently with what has been mentioned above. Extreme activists will not change their opinion even if the issue they target is solved, because it is in the core of their personal ideology and they will not have something to fight for.

Foreign agents

There is no question that foreign powers interfere in the politics of other countries and attempt to meddle in their elections. That's what the secret services are for and it is a part of the geopolitical counterbalancing and a struggle for international domination. The stronger a country is, the more it will try to mediate in situations vital for its overall strategy.

Legally speaking, any foreign citizen or organization actively involved in another country's affairs can be perceived as a foreign agent. It is a vague description because influencing election can be interpreted in many different ways. Any actions of this nature are usually backed by foreign governments with geopolitical interests related to a particular election.

There are three major tools that can be used by external powers to involve themselves in another country's elections:

- **Foreign activists** - Individuals who are not citizens involved in the election process, often driven by their own beliefs.

- **Foreign backed NGOs/Foreign state-backed media networks** - The most common and efficient way for a foreign government or organization to influence and implement geopolitical propaganda.

- **Undercover spies** - While the two mentioned above are overt and often registered as foreign agents, spies have to infiltrate without being detected by local secret services.

Foreign interference is a huge topic worthy of a separate book. This topic is heavily related to geopolitical balance where spheres of influence overlap. Superpowers, regional powers and small countries, they have different objectives and ways to block their adversary's actions. It is easier to negotiate from a position of power, but that can also mean that more influential countries can experience more negative sentiment.

Luckily, international trade agreements and fear of conflict force diplomats and leaders to talk to each other, even when their elections are being targeted by foreign forces. That said, the sole reason any country's secret services exist is to do the same and counterattack from the outside. The only difference between different secret services is their budgets and any domestic laws that limit their control. Spies are not usually too related to the election process itself, more so they are used for sabotage operations and to gather critical information behind 'enemy lines'.

When a foreign power attempts to interfere in another country's election, they are not really trying to help one or another party but follow their agenda which is dictated by domestic and international political concerns. A candidate can weaponize such events by publicly accusing opponents of collaboration with 'enemies of the state'. With a pinch of propaganda and skillful misinformation, doubt might be seeded in voters' minds, even when all accusations are based on assumptions.

Candidates whose party is not in power can benefit from collaborating with think tanks, foundations and other non-government organizations. These can often represent the political views of large groups, usually foreign governments, oligarchies and elites. By officially supporting candidates, such groups can give the masses the perception that research shows that they are intellectuals and the right person to vote for. The backing of such organizations might secure a steady financial flow toward campaigns or leak information when their agenda matches a candidate's profile.

Plan of action

Before looking into the actual election process, let's wrap everything up by discussing a bit about the general strategy for the upcoming 'battle'. As expected, primarily it is a game of winning people's 'hearts and minds' but another key part of the battle is to make the opponent look worse. It's not about winning all the votes; it's about winning enough votes to achieve your goals. In some cases, it might not be about winning more votes but decreasing the number of votes for the opposition.

Policy or strategy? One must lead the campaign. Ideally, there should be a master plan for all events that will most likely take place, but there must always be a backup plan in case things backfire or don't work as expected. Think of the plan not as a straight line, but as a tree, the trunk being the starting point.

If we split the process of a successful candidacy, candidates should divide their projected campaign into three primary steps:

• **Build support** - Strategists should aim to secure a favorable and potentially beneficial political environment for their candidates. Candidates should test the people's reaction to widely popular policies and stick to them if the response is good and doesn't affect the interests of their donors.

• **Distance yourself from troublemakers** - Candidates should stay away from potentially damaging people and groups when there is a high risk that they can negatively affect approval ratings. Moreover, troublemakers might even need to be disavowed or publicly slammed.

• **Work on the next one** - If everything seems lost and the campaign is almost certainly going to fail, the smartest move would be to start preparing for the next election cycle.

Strategists should follow turnout patterns and demographic changes. Although actively changing trends is almost impossible, any party could gain a solid strategic advantage in the future by planning its actions and implementing solutions accordingly. Regarding the present election cycle, it's pure mathematics; as a rule, when the party's core voters are well-empowered and united but the opposition is winning the swing voters, the campaign should not promote mass voting too strongly. And vice versa, when a party has wide support but big chunks of voters are dispersed 'here and there', usually the best idea is to push for a higher turnout. There are 'soft' and 'hard' turnover manipulation methods. Either a party can focus solely on campaigning or promote legislation to change accessibility to the ballots, such as changing the legal age to vote or citizen ownership conditions.

Campaigns can fix a party's image problems by addressing legislative topics of national importance. Rebranding a party is necessary to reestablish themselves on the political field, especially if the predecessors have lost touch with the common voter. This will make the party appeal more to the middle ground, especially for swing voters. However, in doing so there is a risk of pushing away core voters and party activists.

The simplest messages work best for the general public; it is often hard for people to follow complex strategies and they can easily get confused or demotivated. However, candidates should be able to adjust or slightly change the policies they adopt in different situations. Things will come up along the way, and if candidates are too stiff their campaign can get hurt. Candidates might even attempt to brand certain policies in their name. They should know their limits, though, because straight-forward policies might damage a candidate's relations with special interest groups, which could potentially hurt the campaign's fundraising targets.

Moreover, attacking or shutting down some sectors of the economy might be extremely beneficial for a candidate's opponents, as new institutional alliances might arise against such policies. Things can get even worse when such actions create conditions for unemployment, which can potentially push away voters. It is highly unlikely a candidate will gain the support of people who were fired on their watch. Typically, during an election, the smallest groups of society do not matter much, except in cases where large parts of society might feel sympathy for them.

Candidates should be thinking not just about attracting new voters, but also demotivating demographics where their opponent is shown to have higher ratings. Candidates should aim to make most voters feel threatened about something related to the opponent, while at the same time encouraging core voters to cement their support of the party. Many other methods can be used in a campaign battle, but the long-term effects on a country using them might be unpredictable.

A far-sighted politician should be able to see the right moment to stop and take a break from escalating issues further, while at the same time gaining the most of a situation. The same applies to party HQ. Leadership should reevaluate and reassess issues that could be too controversial, reform in a timely manner and prevent the organization from potentially breaking to pieces or heavily lose the election. Without having some form of dialogue, the worst-case scenario for escalations is civil war.

Chapter 4: Elections as an Industry

A simple rule to remember: one person, one vote. No group of voters should be thought less of in terms of intelligence, never base your thoughts on stereotypes and don't get cocky. One vote can have a big impact if voter turnout is low. For example, if only 10% of eligible voters go to the ballots and they all vote for one party, the party will get 100% of the votes and full control of the branches of power in the country.

It starts before it starts: elections are usually a never-ending cycle and they can feel different when candidates come from the party in power to candidates who don't. The more a candidate's face is out there and recognizable, the more identifiable they are going to be with the public which, in turn, can increase a positive perception of them and their approval rating. And we should never forget that the election is an industry itself; many people make money from the election process through advertising, sources of information, business, consultants working on exposure/popularity, and other materials.

There are certain rules unique to each country and any campaign should be designed with them in mind. An electoral college makes the popular vote largely irrelevant and vice versa. In heavily centralized governments, local elections are usually insignificant and not a priority. Rank-choice voting is a whole new story. Also, the point of joining a race is not always to win: a party might be practicing or preparing future candidates, testing tactics, simply looking to get representation on an agenda, and many other reasons. Under authoritarian rule or in cases where a candidate is extremely well-supported (results above 60%), elections are just a technical procedure. The opposition either doesn't exist or has no chance whatsoever.

Campaign trail

Every step a candidate takes must be focused and have a purpose to successfully advance their campaign and hinder their opponent's. As mentioned before, candidates don't necessarily have to believe what they say, as a matter of fact, they rarely do, but it should fit into a scalable idea people are familiar with. Usually, this model can be found and adopted by analyzing past events of successful campaigns that fit with the ideology the candidate is trying to create or emulate.

Candidates with strong majority support of the public usually get better results from positive campaigns, while the opposition should focus on running a negative campaign - highlighting the failures of the party in power. It all gravitates around three words: cause, slogan, name. These are what campaigners need to put together, a summarization of the campaign. The only thing a candidate needs to do is market them in any way possible, branding themselves with the campaign.

Any successful campaign should be focused heavily on three main activities:

•	**Raising money** - Funding a campaign is a never-ending story as expenses usually rise exponentially for candidates that manage to get into the latest stages of the political race.

•	**Participating in events** - Political rallies, media and social events are necessary for any campaign to pick up steam. They position the more proactive candidates in a more favorable situation. Inactive campaigners rarely travel, and they miss out because sometimes all they need is a few events to change the polls.

•	**Getting endorsements** -	Experts, politicians, celebrities and other public figures backing up a candidate is the third vital component to boost a campaign.

Emotions and spontaneity should be controlled during the campaign. Candidates that are too spontaneous can be a pain for their teams and their actions can severely disrupt their original plans. Spontaneous actions can kill a campaign unless the candidate is very charismatic, or their opponents are very weak. There is a line to be followed, which is often dictated by the party backing the candidate.

One of the first things a candidate should do is differentiate themselves to stand out, especially if the field is crowded during the pre-selection stages. This is a time when it really matters who gets exposure and who fits into the party HQ's political agenda. Party HQ can make some candidates look more powerful by creating publicity stunts or giving their chosen candidate momentum by setting them up against weaker candidates who have no chance of winning. Typically, these weaker candidates lack debating skills or even political experience.

Candidates should be careful when partnering or agreeing with other candidates from their own party on vital issues. Focusing on vital issues can assist candidates in getting sympathy from core voters, however, if these issues are typically associated with the party, it can wear down the candidate's unique identity. Moreover, candidates who do not defend widely popular policies aimed at swing voters are simply leaving a vacuum for someone who will.

Candidates can't represent everyone or stand behind every good policy because many policies oppose each other and this spreads candidates thin. Drastically changing political messages when targeting different groups of voters will make candidates look not only stupid but also reveal that they are obviously liars. The trick is to alter a political message in accordance with the concerns of the people or invent issues to fit in with recent developments, while still staying true to the campaign's policies.

Apart from the battle for swing voters, for a successful campaign, candidates need to fire up their base. And here comes the need for strategists to find a suitable but controversial topic; something for people to fight for, a new agenda to push via the media and make a mass appearance. By making people care, candidates will always have a solid group of core voters. If strategists implement this strategy in the right way, any discussion or facts won't matter anymore, and the candidate will have a good number of devoted followers. Candidates can then create different narratives such as villainizing specific groups of people or fabricating the idea of an external enemy. These narratives don't need to be entirely true when implemented in the proper way.

Strategists should start digging for dirt the moment an opponent starts being a real treat. Best case scenario would be to smear or label the opponent based on real facts, though they are not always necessary. With that in mind, it is vital not to cross certain lines because it is possible to unintentionally boost the opponent's campaign when attacks become too harsh. Putting the opponent against the people has a stronger impact on people's perception and strategists can explore this option by using paid protesters when the activists are not active enough.

The alternative to the candidate should be made to look dark and evil, as well as their ideology. That could easily be accompanied by playing with voters' emotions because most people don't think about the bigger picture or related issues. A good team of strategists will be able to find out as much as possible about the most probable opponents beforehand, personality profile, personal and political goals, concerns and fears.

Candidates should ignore opponents with limited exposure and small support, as engaging them means recognizing and giving them a stage. Under no circumstances should a candidate's campaign mention their opponents, and when it comes to political issues, they should be only critical or simply not mention their opponents at all. One of the major mistakes a candidate can make is meet core electorate voters that support their opponent. It is almost impossible for them to be convinced to switch sides and losing a debate with a common citizen can be a complete campaign failure. Meeting 'real' people, in general, can sometimes be a real disaster for politicians, especially for candidates with poor charisma.

Speaking of charisma, most voters are turned off by politicians who constantly talk about statistics, though some are able to break this mold. Candidates should find creative ways to frame positive past policies and legislations so that they benefit themselves, even when they had nothing to do with making them. Utilizing popular talking points or clichés is an easy way to dodge unwanted questions, but unless this is an authoritarian regime, someone will call it out, which can damage a candidate's credibility.

Candidates not only need strong financial backing, but they also need to find the 'right beds to get into'. Political coalitions, lobbying, endorsements, and even international relations are some of the ways to secure enough support for a potentially successful campaign. What they will be required to provide in return depends on the balance of power and their capabilities. Rewarding people for their loyalty with an 'upgrade' in status is a big part of the game - national heroes, knighthoods, appointments to key positions, etc.

Candidates also need to make 'friends' with celebrities to get more exposure. Like candidates, celebrities don't have to believe in everything they say, but they must look like they do. A crucial thing about this though is that they must somehow fit in with the campaign, otherwise the whole endeavor will look fake. Ideally, people who endorse a candidate should be able to give the candidate access to voters they may not have. They are in a sense buying a market. Additionally, celebrities can be used to solidify a candidate's hold on core voters who should not be taken for granted. The opposition will be seeking to weaken a candidate's hold on core voters too, so their opinion must not be swayed.

The campaign must follow its planned direction, but strategists should leave room for adjustments. There should be a team of analysts who observe the campaign's effectiveness. They, in turn, will be able to see what kind of actions might have a positive effect on voter perception and which do not. To achieve an adequate level of flexibility, they should follow every step of the campaign, every debate, news story and every tour.

Debates

Getting debates right is vital for candidates. Debates are an opportunity for candidates to directly face their opponent's frontrunner and put their ideas on display in front of many viewers. How the competitors are portrayed, and the difficulty of the questions asked by moderators is directly linked to who owns the media that broadcast the debate. Regardless of how biased the debate is and the underlying interests of the media, debates are always great press coverage.

Candidates must emit a sense of leadership, even when they lack leadership skills; they cannot afford to look like a puppet. One easy mistake to make at this stage is to unintentionally destroy the illusion that a candidate is in charge.

However, what the viewers of the debate are about to witness is likely to be a less-controlled version of the candidate and so charisma is a significant advantage. Candidates need to rest and look fresh on debate day as the nation will be watching.

Candidates who lack debating skills and are unable to argue their points will struggle immensely. Thus, a proven track record of debating is ideal. Before starting a campaign, when a candidate is new to the game, they should start making their presence known by getting involved in small-scale debates or local discussions. The topic won't matter much to party HQ, the only goal of these debates would be to provide the potential candidate with experience and get their face known.

For better performance in debates, there are few steps to be followed:

• **Do not miss an opportunity to speak** - When given an opportunity to speak, candidates shouldn't pause and must stop only when they are forced to stop.

• **Never agree with opponents** - Candidates should distinguish themselves from their opponents and, even if they are on an issue, they should shift their own perspective a bit (but not flip on it) to make it unique. By agreeing with an opponent, a candidate is essentially advertising their opponent's policies and points of view.

• **Back claims with examples** - An example makes a point of view more credible, but they need to be true, even when they are exceptional cases. When candidates don't have facts or statistics on their side, they can speak about marginal cases and give the public only half the facts or hide inconvenient details.

When on the offense, candidates should be careful not to go too far and be colored as an aggressor. They can afford to insult their opponents under certain conditions, but never the voters behind them. In the best-case scenario, the craftiest candidates will find a way to pitch their opponents against the public. With that in mind, taking insults too far can be problematic and can look quite bad in the eyes of swing voters.

It is critical for candidates to put a negative spin on their opponents' good policies and accomplishments unless they are simply too good to be denied. When their opponent has achieved something extraordinary, candidates should try to downplay these triumphs, when possible. Calling out opponents for bad decisions they may or may not have made is also a potentially beneficial approach and can lead them to blurt out excuses, which can make them look weak. Ideally, a candidate shouldn't be making excuses, but their opponent should. A candidate's end goal should be to anger their opponents, in an attempt to unravel the ugly looking side of certain personalities.

Candidates should choose the right moment to misdirect or divert attention, as well as how. Avoiding a question multiple times can be read by the public as an obvious sign of covering something up, lying, or, even worse, incompetence. It is important to understand until what point diverting attention is an option and when it is time to come clean.

During a debate, if the opposition is highly skilled, candidates shouldn't go too deep into topics and should avoid escalating them. After a debate, a candidate might attack the opposition when the risk of looking weak is lower. However, if there is an issue that could escalate the situation but it is based on fact, then the candidate has no other choice but to attempt to show the audience how their opponent's points of view are wrong and out of touch with reality. The ability to withstand pressure and not quit after the first few setbacks is critical, especially for direct clashes with political rivals.

Candidates must look like their campaign can answer any question voters might have. Ideally, they should have a response to everything, a logical train of thought voters can follow. This is especially true for yes-no questions, which can be a trap. A candidate's rivals should always be made to look like bad or crazy people, defending devastating policies. Candidates should avoid topics related to their opponents' success and purposely misinterpret their statements related to policies supported by the masses, or at least parts of them. Covering topics that are usually dominated by an opponent is a reasonable step only when candidates have a clear plan and objectives or there is no general consensus by the public on the point in question.

Arguments must be strongly formed as they will be dissected by political commentators in many different mediums. Analysts will look for anything that fits into their interpretation of what the candidate argues, all the way down to their body language. Candidates should be well-prepared, careful and avoid words that could be self-destructive and cause a backlash as mentioned above (unless it's a trap for opponents or part of a bigger plan). The following day, quotes will be taken and printed in newspapers, sometimes with the context removed. But the beauty of the debates is that live TV can't be edited while broadcasting.

Scandals

Controversy and hypocrisy are only bad when associated with the 'other side'; core voters tend to excuse the same situations if reversed. There are many different types of scandals, some can be recovered from, some cannot. Sometimes it only takes one stupid mistake, one stupid word, to kill an entire campaign. Funny enough, the scandal itself is not that dangerous, regardless of its scale. An inappropriate reaction to the scandal from a candidate can be much worse.

The most important thing to remember about scandals is that they reveal that someone's moral character is not what it originally seemed. This can be used by opponents to demonstrate that the candidate was lying to the people the whole time and they should withdraw their trust in this politician. That said, if a scandal was made public years before, it is likely that the candidate has either been forgiven for their actions, exonerated from any bad doing or voters just don't care too much anymore.

The most important part of a scandal is when it is made public. The most damaging time is during the election itself. At this point, it doesn't matter if it is an ongoing scandal or something that happened years before but was only recently discovered.

If claims are not backed by facts and evidence, a scandal can backfire badly. That's why it's safer to use a proxy, another (political) figure to look like an aggressor. This person might be driven by personal beliefs, has nothing to lose or is chosen by the party HQ to be the scapegoat. For a scandal to have a greater impact, strategists need to find a way to make it viral and spark a reaction in voters and especially activists, leading to demonstrations and kompromats publicized in the media.

It is possible for the attacked side to spin the scandal and end up portraying their candidate in a positive light. If so, the scandal has failed and can be turned into a mass scale counterattack and increase support for their candidate. Also, looking for scandals in the private lives of opponents might look like an unethical attack in the eyes of the voters.

There is a list of critical no-nos for candidates when hit with a major scandal:

•   **Candidates shouldn't try to hide** - There is no point in hiding anything that is publicly available. The moment it's out there is no point for the candidates to deny it.

•   **Candidates shouldn't apologize** - The moment candidates apologize, they admit wrongdoing in the eyes of the public. This is a huge no-no for a campaign.

•   **Candidates shouldn't stay on the topic** - Public opinion should be distracted as soon as possible by all means; misleading or fabricating an issue and arguing against it, for example.

There are numerous ways to get out of scandals. Well-liked candidates can sometimes walk away from scandals unscathed, while less likeable candidates can find it difficult. Apologizing is political suicide and can kill a campaign, especially if a candidate spends a lot of time doing it. Repeatedly apologizing can make a candidate look weak and regretful of their decisions. Ideally, candidates should look confident and do something to counteract the negative labels attached to them, not feed them. When a candidate knows the source of an attack, it would be worth showing some muscle and attempting to reverse it.

It would be better for a candidate to admit their part in a scandal at the beginning than deny it and get caught or apologize later. Acknowledging the existence of scandal shows sincerity and at the same time is not necessarily an apology. Another way to handle a scandal is to do nothing about it. A candidate's best chance might be to ride it out and pretend that it never happened. People tend to forget, hopefully, this time it will happen again.

Corruption scandals are perhaps the worst possible kind of scandal for a candidate to be involved in as it is highly suggestive that the candidate's goals are not the same as the voters. To voters, it suggests that the candidate is only in politics for money. Candidates who have ever been involved in corruption will always have a hard time convincing voters that they can be trusted. People hate it when bureaucrats steal taxpayer money, even though they will never see the candidate again. Openly corrupt staff members can also be very damaging to any election campaign.

The favorite of tabloids, affairs can be most damaging when they lead to the collapse of a candidate's family. It conveys a sense of recklessness. Additionally, the media can end up portraying the candidate as lustful and selfish. In some situations, it is possible for a candidate to continue campaigning after an affair has been made public, for example, if it happened years before. However, if a candidate loses their family due to an affair, it is highly likely they will step out of the race.

Use of drugs and other substances is another common scandal that could swing a campaign. Depending on the kind of substance, this can have a varying effect. Weaker drugs can sometimes be dismissed, while hard drugs can lead voters to question the candidate's ability to lead. Again, this also depends on when the candidate was using. If it took place many years ago, it can be forgiven. If it is ongoing, most likely voters will not forgive it. It is worth mentioning though, if the candidate is a fully recovered addict, this can add a level of character to them that most other candidates do not have, making their profile more human and relatable

Regardless of the scandal type, the worst possible scenario would be for it to spiral out of control. If nothing works and the campaign is ruined anyway, a candidate can attempt to make the best out of it; quitting at the right moment can make them a cult hero and boost all future events related to the candidate.

Political games

The best political strategists think of the election from a wider perspective. They know that their turn in office is just part of the cycle, part of something bigger that is interconnected to domestic and foreign trends. The complex mixture of interconnected processes and people might lead to paradoxical scenarios where elected officials have basically no legislative power or only a small group of appointed people have total control on all key decisions related to the country.

Elections are important, no doubt, but not as much as the level of centralization/decentralization, as well as who controls the branches of power and who appoints judges/ambassadors, etc. Under certain conditions and circumstances, certain people might have enormous political influence on vital processes in the country even when they are not officially in power. In the meantime, public support should be maintained, as winning a majority leaves room for changing the rules.

There is always a reason behind critical actions such as blocking or vetoing bills, impeachment procedures, snap elections and referendums, for example. It usually comes down to those in charge seeking to concentrate power and weaken any sources of power for those who would like to take control. The advantage (or disadvantage) of the party in power is that voters can see the consequences of their governance, while the opposition is usually an enigma and the results are yet to be seen.

To fully utilize every aspect of society, strategists attempt to find new ways to merge politics with popular activities or beliefs in order to weaponize them. However, heavily mixing politics with entertainment, sports, religion or brands can become problematic, because after a certain point people begin to realize that it is being used as a propaganda tool, which can lead them to distance themselves.

A landslide victory sounds like a good thing, but when the party doesn't have a strong ideological opponent, core voters can get bored. Strategists and experts should recognize if a major rival party is collapsing and fractured beyond repair. As a next step, the most common way for parties to avoid unexpected political movements (both internal and external) and keep their own base active, is to design a controlled opposition according to their needs. To have a limited impact on swing voters, it is a good idea for such political projects to be positioned leaning towards ideological extremes. Ideally, proxy party leaders won't even realize their true purpose.

Speaking of metamorphosis, in cases where two major parties create a permanent coalition or have unanimous bipartisan support on too many issues critical for society, it can create a political vacuum. You can't combine salt and sugar and expect something good to happen. Moreover, most people might see it as an attempt by the establishment to cement themselves to power.

When a party holds a large ideological block of voters who start pushing in a certain direction, it can dissuade swing voters or create conditions that can lead to a crisis in party identity, which can disenfranchise some core voters. This, in turn, gives the opportunity for alternative radical parties to rise and find their support from disappointed voters.

People can get angry because of many different things and sometimes it is hard to predict an upcoming political crisis. 'Quiet voters' rarely speak to polling agencies and the media can get the wrong idea of the real situation by only reporting loud voices. It is almost impossible to find a balance, because there are no policies everybody can agree with. Too many rules and unnecessary laws can be harmful to the economy and people's way of life, but no regulation can mean heavy decentralization, which can cause minority rights issues and increased separatist movements.

In the end, somebody always has to lose. The party can create numerous excuses and blame whoever they like but losing is losing. How far they will be willing to go to fight a loss depends on the power and tools of influence they have. Actions could vary from mobilizing activists, attempts to delegitimize an election and even to calls for revolution. A party that has been in power for too long without being challenged may express an extreme reaction to losing. Similarly, steadily growing movements that have never experienced a loss may also be shocked.

Chapter 5: Outro

Politics is the art of lying and finding various excuses for unfulfilled promises. The question, however, quite often comes down to the individuals who control large sections of the economy. Because the economy is the 'engine' of the country that pumps the financial system, without it, the country cannot function. If you want to understand the logic behind any major political shift, just follow the money.

The desire for power and unwillingness to let go of influence can be limited (to an extent) by balancing central leadership with other branches of power. Balance is the key to any stable political system, as a heavy decentralization could be equally (if not more) damaging for a country and its people.

During the first term after winning an election, a party is usually more grounded in reality and aware of different possibilities. However, holding on to power for too long can lead politicians to lose their way. Their personality could shift from egotistical to arrogant, which can change everything related to the ruling classes' ideological direction. In reality, though, blocking centralization is usually done because lawmakers are afraid to lose their own positions and influence in politics. I strongly advise you not to idealize any political movements or ideologies, because regardless of the power structure or terms of office, things can change, and sometimes even 'good' ideas might be implemented in a wrong way.

Bureaucracy and corruption are always going to be there, regardless of the regime type or social order. People are people and many are driven by greed: give them the means to enrich themselves and most won't be able to resist. Speaking about personality types, another specific group to mention are 'overly ideological' radicals driven by their principles. Often aggressive, they might poison any 'party message' to moderates if their influence or power grows too much.

Whoever takes power can potentially adjust the vector of the country and even manipulate history through simple propaganda. Textbooks are to be approved and written by the 'winners'. But by 'supporting your side no matter what' the situation with meaningless or extreme statements could radicalize the opposition's stance and will push away swing voters. Double standards and hypocrisy can deepen divisions even more and then it is just a matter of time before things get violent.

There is no universal formula where everyone is happy, especially in politics. An election is the choice of the masses and sometimes your party/candidate loses. It doesn't matter if the candidate is not very popular when they have more votes than everyone else or if they manage to successfully form a coalition.

www.ingramcontent.com/pod-product-compliance
Lightning Source LLC
Chambersburg PA
CBHW070818280726
48660CB00016B/2125